PREDATOR IN
A DRESS

A MAN'S GUIDE TO ESCAPING THE BRUTAL UNFAIRNESS
OF DIVORCE IN AMERICA

Greg Mulligan

Author's Tranquility Press
ATLANTA, GEORGIA

Greg Mulligan/Author's Tranquility Press
3900 N Commerce Dr. Suite 300 #1255
Atlanta, GA 30334, USA
www.authorstranquilitypress.com

Ordering Information:
Quantity sales. Special discounts are available on quantity purchases by corporations, associations, and others. For details, contact the "Special Sales Department" at the address above.

Predator in a Dress /Greg Mulligan
Paperback: 978-1-963636-72-7
eBook: 978-1-963636-73-4

Contents

Introduction

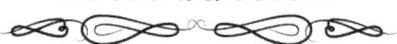

Some women get married just so they can get divorced. They are after child support, spousal maintenance, a nice car and a nice house. Women who do this are a type of con artist. "Predator in a dress" is an appropriate name for them.

Our court system rewards women who treat marriage as a way to make money. The courts award women money for getting divorced. More money if they were unemployed during the marriage. Even more if they have some children from the marriage. Even more money if a nanny watched the children all day. All of this money is supplied by the ex-husband, whether he can spare it or not. The purpose of this book is to arm men with the knowledge needed to protect themselves from the gross unfairness of divorce laws in America. Every day, in every state in the country, men with good hearts and good incomes are converted into bitter men in financial ruin because they were victimized by divorce laws, and by wives who married them just so they could divorce them soon after.

A substantial percentage of women use marriage as a tool to drain money from men. These predatory women have their plan in place long before they ever meet their future husband. At the foundation of the predators' plan is American divorce law.

Greg Mulligan

The women who run these plans are everywhere. They are difficult to spot. A good woman can even be converted into one of them by a friend, by her mother, or by her lawyer. Every man owes a duty to himself and his children to protect himself from the damage these women can do.

Chapter One

The Foundation of the Predators' System

Child custody rules form the foundation of the predator's system. She knows she has to win custody of the children in order for the money to really start flowing her way. She knows how to win a custody hearing. She goes to her custody hearing knowing exactly what she has to show the judge in order to win. She tells the judge exactly what he wants to know without using up his time on anything else. She wins custody. In a divorce, the parent who wins custody of the children gets the house, a car, and a monthly child support check. Maybe even Spousal Maintenance. These are the prizes the con artist/bride is after.

Here is the con artists' plan: First, find a mark. A man with lots of money. Maybe a doctor, engineer, or accountant. Maybe a carpenter who doesn't mind working overtime. Shower him with attention and then affection. Before long he will fall in love and propose marriage. After the wedding, pick out a nice house and move in. Have a couple of children and convince the mark of the importance and value of a stay-at-home mom. Stay at home to raise your children. As the kids grow and learn, use the time alone with them to teach them to always come to Mommy when they get hurt, because Mommy is good at "taking care of owies". Teach them to wake Mommy up if they are ever sick in the night. They should let their Dad sleep because he gets angry if anything wakes him up. Always make trips to the doctor fun by singing "The Doctor Song" along the way to ease tension and make trips to see the doctor with Mommy fun.

When things are ripe for the divorce to be filed, ask the mark for a trip to Europe or a new and bigger house. If he delivers, delay the divorce. After the Mark has had all of his money squeezed out of him, the divorce action can be filed. During the proceedings, paint a glorious picture of yourself for the judge. At the custody hearing answer "Me!" to each of the "Three Questions of Custody" and win custody of the children. (The "Three Questions of Custody" are: 1) "Who takes the children to the doctor?" 2) "Who stays up in the night with the kids when they are sick?" and 3) "Who do the kids run to when they skin their knee?"

The judge will decide that the children will be better off together, in their house, and with their Mom. The Husband will be ordered to leave. If he is homeless, that is too bad. He has to send his ex-wife child support equal to 1/3 of his income and Spousal Maintenance, also equal to 1/3 of his income. Both payments will continue until the youngest child turns 18 and graduates High School.

After the divorce is complete, Look up to the sky and yell: "What a great country!"

Nice plan, eh? That very plan has been working over and over again for years. The reason men don't know about it is because, 1) Women know better than to talk about it and kill the goose that lays the golden eggs and, 2) Men don't talk about it because it is embarrassing to have your wife walk out on you. The victim of this con thinks he is the only one.

If you would like to get married without having to fund a plan like this, you need to pay attention to clues you might get while dating (see chapter 5). If you missed all the clues while dating, watch for the clues that appear after the honeymoon (Ch.5), which are a little more obvious. If you realize you have fallen for the marriage con, employ the steps described in Chapter 7 and see if you can avoid financial disaster.

If you have kids, make sure they know that they can wake you up in the night anytime they don't feel good. Tell them to come and show you anytime they get hurt. Make sure that you go to the doctor with the kids every time they go. Make sure there is an ice cream stop after every doctor visit. Then you will win custody in the event that your wife divorces you. Receiving child support is a lot better than paying it.

Gentlemen, answer the three questions "Me, Me and Me" and you have no need to fear divorce court anymore.

Uninformed men don't stand a chance against the marriage con. Most men have no idea the scheme even exists. They have no idea they will be in a custody hearing one day. Most men have no idea how the judge will decide the custody issue. They have no idea what the three questions of custody are. The con artist knows all of the above. She goes into this fight well prepared. She hand picks her victim. It's like a pro boxer going to a bar and picking a fight with a drunk. Everybody knows how it's going to end.

But not for you! You now have the knowledge needed to escape that fate. You are not going to marry a predator. If you do, you are going to win custody if your marriage ends in divorce. Justice will actually prevail in your case. Even if justice does not prevail, you will have enough secret savings to allow you to have a decent standard of living after the divorce is all over. You will not be wiped out like so many men have been before.

Below is a list of legal rules (some official, some unofficial) pertaining to divorce. Every man should know this stuff. If you are going to be married, you need to know the rules. If men can learn the rules of the fight, all of a sudden, the con artist doesn't have such an easy time of it anymore. Suddenly men are not paying child support, they are not losing their house and they are not a victim of any con-artist.

East Coast women learn these rules when they are teenagers. The same way men taught you how to fish and play baseball, some woman taught your wife or future wife about the benefits of divorce and how to win a custody battle.

THE RULES:

1. If a married couple has a house and young child, upon divorce the parent who gets custody of the children also gets the house. She also gets a car, child support, and spousal maintenance.

2. The wife will almost always win custody of the children. This is half because Judges are biased in favor of women and half because men have no idea how to win a child custody hearing. Men don't know how they

will cope as a single father. Women learn this information as teenagers. You are learning it now.

3. If a single woman wants a nice house with a nice car, spousal maintenance and child support payments, all she has to do is marry a man with money, move into a house with him and have some children. She impersonates a wife and mother for a few years and then divorces her husband. If she likes kids, it's a really good deal.

4. Judges are biased in favor of women.

5. The judge will keep the children together and in the house. If the wife gets custody, the Judge will award the house to the wife. The judge will not complicate the case by requiring the sale of the house when the kids graduate High School. The Judge will award the wife full title to the house, as her share of the marital property, in the Final Decree.

The Court almost never splits the property evenly. The party with the biggest income gets less property. If the family's only substantial asset is the home equity, then the wife gets the family's only substantial asset. This is why the con artists are always lobbying their husbands for a bigger, more expensive house. The con-artist wants to divert all of her husband's earnings into the one asset she knows she is going to get.

Have you ever known a couple with a perfectly nice house who moved so they could get a bigger house? This is the mark of a predator. I'll bet the wife holds sex hostage for ransom all the time. The husband agreed to buy her the new house in hopes of finally getting some sex from his now happy wife. Good luck!

6. Fairness is NOT required in Divorce Court.

7. There are THREE questions the Judge asks in a custody hearing. 1) Who takes the kids to see the doctor? 2) Who stays up in the night with the kids when they are sick? and 3) Who do the kids go to when they get hurt?

IF YOUR WIFE CAN ANSWER THESE THREE QUESTIONS "ME, ME, and ME" SHE WINS CUSTODY AND <u>YOU</u> GET THE KIDS EVERY OTHER WEEKEND. You lose your house and all the equity, you lose your favorite car, you pay child support and spousal maintenance. They take your savings and your retirement nest egg. You are left in financial ruin at age 41 or 52 knowing you can never fully recover from what the Court has done to you. The one thing that keeps you from being a total loss is your kids and you only get to see them every other weekend.

You ask "How the hell did this happen to me?" This happens because a set of laws were put into place which were designed to protect good women from bad men. The system presumes all men are bad and all women are good. A Divorce action is like a weapon available to any woman to use on any man she can get to marry her. Courts in America make no effort to protect men from financial destruction. They watch it happen every day. Con artists who use marriage and divorce to make easy money can rely on this avenue being open forever. Don't get steamrolled by this system. Actively protect yourself from it.

Chapter Two

Marriage as a Con Job

Marriage can be a simple con job. A shrewd woman meets a trusting man with money and the woman immediately goes to work. If she has got a live one, in four or five years she might be waving goodbye to him from inside the house he bought for her. The predator in a dress is most commonly found in the Northeast United States. However, they are becoming more and more common everywhere.

When the con artist has married her mark, after the honeymoon, the con artist routinely withholds sex from the mark unless he complies with her every request. She requests an expensive house and children (Note: Once she has the house and kids, she has succeeded. The only question is "How much can she take him for?"). She requests his blessing to quit working and stay home to care for the children. She requests more money than the mark can earn. She requests jewelry and clothing and luxurious vacations, she requests unlimited credit cards (Never agree to that!), she requests servants to keep up the house so she can "focus on the children". Then she requests a Nanny so she can "get some things done around here" (Yes, the stay-at-home wife wants a nanny and Yes "Get things done around here" is code for "go shopping"). Next, she asks for a bigger, better house in an expensive neighborhood. Once the con artist has gotten as much out of the mark as he can produce, she cuts off all sex. She stops pretending to love him. The con artist tells her husband (the mark) that her lack of affection for him is his fault because he does not "communicate" or "consider her feelings" and he does not adequately "nurture their relationship". The mark will then either increase his efforts to please the con artist or give up.

Eventually, most marks give up. Once that happens, the con has run its course and the con artist divorces the mark. Divorce laws of all 50 states will place something between 50% and 100% of the marital assets in the wife's hands. She will get the house, all the furniture, a car, custody of the children and child support until the youngest child turns 18. She will get spousal maintenance longer than that. She will then be free to run the same con job on another mark. The entire process takes from 4 to 70 years. Some men stop meeting the con artist's demands after a couple of years. Some men continue handing all of their money to the con artist their entire life.

By far, the most important elements of the scheme are 1) Convincing the Mark to buy the most expensive house he can leverage them into, 2) Have children, and 3) Win the custody battle. Divorce laws make it this way.

Chapter Three

How a man can win custody and come out ahead in his divorce.

Con artists know lots of cons. Every con is different but they share certain elements. Every one requires that the victim trust and believe the con artist. The marriage con works because divorce laws can be relied on to transfer the mark's wealth to the con artist time after time. Additionally, every successful marriage con requires that the Mark believe that his bride truly loves him and wants to spend her life with him. This is why the marriage con is so cruel. The victim is left with a broken heart as well as being in financial ruin. There is an element of Treason present. There is also the fact that the Judge was a full participant in the affair. This learned professional was thoroughly biased against the victim and in favor of the thief. The victim knew what was happening and the judge disregarded everything the victim said. It is hard to imagine greater frustration.

Unfortunately, no one is going to save any man from the marriage con. Judges won't do it. Friends and family rarely know the fiancé well enough to know she is a con artist. If a man is going to be saved from a predator in a dress, he has to do it himself. A man who wants to win his custody hearing has to win over the judge first.

*** ATTENTION: LEGAL ADVICE***: To win over the judge, a man has to be dignified, respectful and quiet. Don't speak out of turn, don't scream and don't call your ex and her lawyer Liars and other bad names. Instead, only speak when testifying or when the judge addresses you directly. Answer your lawyer's questions, answer the judge's questions. Explain that you always stayed up with the kids if they got sick in the night and you always drove them to the doctor's office. Explain that you are the one the kids come to when they hurt themselves.

Work hard to stay calm. Make the judge think you are a breath of fresh air compared to the average man going through a divorce in his courtroom. The judge will be happy with you for behaving exactly the way he wants you to. He will actually consider your argument and your point of view. Follow this formula and your chances of winning will go up dramatically.

Here is a list of facts about divorce all men need to know:

1. Divorce laws are a tool women can use to make money.

2. Divorce laws typically result in a transfer of all wealth from the ex-husband to the ex-wife. This is the prize the con artist is after.

3. Not only do women get more than half of the couple's property, they get monthly spousal maintenance and child support checks too.

4. The wife does not have to pay for anything in order to get most of everything. A man who argues that he paid for everything so he should get more

property in the divorce decree is wasting his breath.

5. Modern divorce laws came into effect about five minutes before the first con artist planned to get married just so she could get divorced.

6. The divorce laws are punitive to men.

7. Divorce Courts are biased in favor of women. The judges don't even attempt to disguise it.

8. Unpaid child support and spousal maintenance cannot be discharged in bankruptcy. In other words: Even filing bankruptcy won't get you out of paying your child support and spousal maintenance.

9. Police are available at a moment's notice to assist women any time they have a conflict with a man.

10. The woman does not have to spend the child support on the children.

11. Nonpayment of child support or spousal maintenance will land a man in jail for Contempt of Court.

12. It is a fact that the parent who gets custody of the children will get the house, and not just until the kids turn 18. She gets it as her share of the property! Accordingly, the con artist has to make sure of two things. 1) That she talks her husband into buying the most expensive house possible, and 2) That she wins the custody battle.

The divorce laws place the wife in charge and a con artist willing to take advantage of the system has a great tool to work with. She can take all of her husband's property and future income with the full support and assistance of the Court, the legislature, and the Sheriff.

Everything the con artist does is in anticipation of divorce laws and judges supporting her. The con artist knows the rules backwards and forward before her 18th birthday. You need to know them just as well. You need to know how they can be used against you.

Reading the statutes on divorce won't help you predict what the judges will do. Statutes are only a guide to judges. The judges have "Discretion" which allows them to make whatever orders are needed to produce "Justice". The word "Justice" is code for "whatever the judge wants." A judge's decision can only be overturned on appeal if you can show "abuse of discretion" by the judge. This standard of review is almost never met.

If a man has to spend all of his money paying the mortgage, all of the family's wealth will be in the house's equity. Whomever gets the house gets all the family's wealth. This is exactly what the con artist wants. The husband buys her the house in hopes of making her happy and the judge awards her the house to provide security to her and her children. A good con artist fool everybody.

Chapter Four

Are you a Mark?

The best marks for the marriage con have some or all of the following characteristics. The more of these characteristics you have, the better mark you will make.

1. High Annual Income
2. Assets
3. Trusting Nature
4. Loyalty
5. You are a "Good Boy"
6. No Experience with Con Artists
7. No experience with Divorce
8. A Desire to have Children and a Stay-at-Home Wife

1. High Annual Income

    The best mark earns a high income. The mark may currently be a med student or the only child of a wealthy, sick, old man. Wealth in the near future is as good as present wealth. The divorce laws of every state base the amount of child support and spousal maintenance to be awarded on the man's income. The more money the man makes, the more money he will be ordered to pay in child support and spousal maintenance following a divorce. In addition, men with higher incomes can buy bigger houses. A con artist can really make some money divorcing a man who makes a lot of money. Collecting the payments is easy too. Remember this: If he does not pay what the Court orders him to pay, the judge can have him arrested and held in jail for contempt.

2. Assets

Assets are not directly considered by the court in determining child support. They are, however, considered in determining spousal maintenance payments. Assets held before marriage are not officially part of the property that gets divided up in a divorce. However, the more assets a man has, the more able to make child support and spousal maintenance payments he will be. Additionally, courts in every state have the ability to characterize assets as having been converted from non-marital property to marital property. Divorce laws in every state leave room for discretion on the part of the judge in dividing property and awarding support payments. In most states, the judge is free to do literally whatever she wants. All of a man's earnings and assets are up for grabs in a divorce. When judges have discretion, there is room for biased decision making. The assets do not have to be split evenly. They almost never are when the couple has minor children. The fact that the man paid for every asset with the money he earned at work is perfectly irrelevant.

3. A Trusting Nature

This is a vital characteristic of a good mark. The con artist has her best chance for success when dealing with a mark who never suspects a thing. When she looks into his eyes, his heart should melt. He should be willing to trust his true love with his very life. A man with a trusting nature can't conceive of his soul mate ever doing anything to harm him. Trusting men get hit hardest by the marriage con. Trusting a con artist is like standing flat-footed in a boxing match with your guard down. You are going to get clobbered.

4. Loyalty

The mark has to be loyal for the con artist to maximize her take. The main tool used by the con artist is to withhold sex unless she gets what she wants. If the mark is loyal, she can rest assured that he will not seek sex and affection from other women. The con artist loses the ability to squeeze money out of a mark when he is getting sex from another woman. If the mark cannot be squeezed for money any longer, the con artist has to conclude the con and divorce the mark. She will tell people that she divorced him for infidelity. The truth is that the con job was not working because holding sex hostage from him was no longer useful.

A telltale sign of a woman who is running the marriage con is extreme jealousy. She watches her husband's eyes every time another woman enters the room. If he so much as looks at the other woman, the con artist throws a fit. Marital fidelity is the single most important thing to a woman running the marriage con. This behavior causes the mark to ask "Why are you so jealous? You don't even like me and you never give me sex. Why would you even care if there was another woman?" If you have ever asked your wife that question, there is probably a custody battle in your future. Your wife is probably running the marriage con on you.

The con artist marries for money. She constantly threatens to withhold sex if she does not get what she wants. Behind the threat of no sex is the threat of divorcing you if you do not obey her. She knows she can make you homeless with one phone call. She talks to you like a servant because that is what you are to her.

Another telltale sign that a woman is running the con is when a woman gives her husband sex exactly once each month. Never more or less. She has been told that once each month is just enough to keep him from leaving her. Obviously, if he leaves, the con is over. These women typically get angry at their husband if he comes anywhere near them on the other days of the month.

5. A "Good Boy"

A "Good Boy" is easier to manipulate than a "Bad Boy". Con Artists can often be seen with "Bad Boys" but they do not marry them. A good boy is one that is kind and generous. He is selfless and helpful. He takes care of his children and watches them while his wife shops. He would never be unfaithful to his wife. He does not get angry or argue with his wife. He does all he can to make her happy. He buys her flowers for no particular reason. She gets presents at every holiday, birthday and anniversary. He does activities that she likes and lets her pick the movie every time. He gets the door, carries her bags, and picks up the tab everywhere they go. He works hard to be every woman's dream come true. He goes to church. He loves his mother, and he would never embarrass her by being unfaithful to his wife. This guy even reads books about how to make his wife happy. Women have a term for such men: Husband Material. Con artists have another term for them: Lunch.

6. No Experience with Con Artists

The mark cannot suspect a thing. Even a trusting soul can become cautious if he has been conned before. A con artist depends upon trust from the victim. Every con of any kind requires the victim's trust. Young people are more trusting but old people have more money. A con artist has a lot to consider when hunting for a good mark.

7. A Desire to have Children and a Stay-at-Home Wife

To a woman running the marriage con, children are the most effective tool to put money in her pocket. In an American divorce, whomever gets custody of the kids gets the house, the best car in the household, the child support and possibly spousal maintenance. To a predator in a dress, children are Money. A woman who does not have kids does not get the house. She does not get child support payments and is less likely to get spousal maintenance. If a childless woman is a stay-at-home wife for many years, she may get spousal maintenance, but not as much as a stay-at-home mom.

If a wife stays at home and "gives up a career" for the husband, she gets rewarded by the Court with an order for Spousal Maintenance. A con artist loves nothing more than a demand from her husband that she stays home and manage the house while he has a career outside the home. Most women would reject such an arrangement. Women planning a future divorce would gladly be a stay-at-home wife.

If you are a single man and you have some or all of the traits listed in this chapter, you are a mark. Take heart though, you are also an excellent catch for a woman who is not a con artist. Since getting married to a good woman is a good thing for you, your future children, and society, I recommend that you hang on to these traits. Every one of them is a virtue. What you should do is hope that your bride is not a con artist and take the steps necessary to protect yourself (see chap.7) in case she is.

Chapter Five

How to Recognize a Predator in a Dress

A. BEFORE the wedding: It is very difficult.

Look for greed. It is the one thing all con artists have in common. A love of expensive jewelry and a belief that it belongs on her wrist and hanging from her ears. Look for wanton spending. Maybe compulsive spending. This type of woman typically owns more outfits and shoes than she could wear in a year. Look for Bankruptcy caused by simply spending more than she earns. Spendthrifts like to spend other peoples' money. If your fiancé has money problems, she may be getting married simply to have her husband pay her debts. Someone who plans a wedding so she can get her hands on someone else's money is exactly the kind of person you need to avoid! A con artist wants to get married before you ever learn about her financial problems. I recommend getting a copy of your fiancé's credit report long before the wedding plans are made. You should take an unofficial inventory of her clothing, shoes, and jewelry too.

A spendthrift often becomes a con artist out of desperation. Someone who stays broke buying junk she does not need or shows an inability to save up for a desired purchase might decide that marriage to a rich man is the way to go. Look for someone who never pays her bills. Never brings her credit card balances to Zero. Look for someone who wants to live way beyond her means. Maybe someone who doesn't mind stealing, maybe even doing a little shoplifting.

B. AFTER the wedding: There are many ways to recognize a con artist.

Prior to the wedding, the con artist can be indistinguishable from a good woman. They can appear to be the same in every way. However, the plans the con artist has make her very different from the others. Obviously, the con artist will not disclose her plans for you prior to the wedding. She won't even admit she conned you after the con is complete. She will deny it as long as she lives. The telltale signs of the con do not even appear until after the honeymoon. Victims of the marriage con will often remark "The woman I was married to had nothing in common with the woman I proposed to". What is more, even a good woman can be converted into a predator by her friends or a divorce lawyer should your marriage to a good woman end in divorce.

The ways to recognize a con artist posing as a loving wife are many. Here is a list of all I know:

1. Once married, she insists on a nice big house in a nice neighborhood. One with a good resale value. She surprises you with her interest in Real Estate. She wants to spend much more than you are comfortable with.

2. Once she is in a house, she insists it is time to have children. [Note: Once she has kids and a house, she owns you. She is going to milk every dollar she can

from you and then divorce you.]

3. Once she has children, she asks to get a bigger, better house in an expensive neighborhood.

4. She says she wants to be a stay-at-home mom. [Note: If you agree to this, get ready to pay half your take home pay in Spousal Maintenance for the rest of your working life.]

5. She wants servants. Gardener, cook, maid, NANNY. Yes, she is a stay-at-home mom and she wants a nanny. [Note: The more servants she has in her life, the more spousal maintenance you will pay. Yes, this does seem backward. You ask "Do the Courts really reward laziness?" Answer: "Yes. Laziness is the one thing they do reward." Judges try to provide the woman with the same standard of living before and after the divorce.

6. If the husband ever says "No" there will be no sex that night, week, or month. She holds sex hostage. You either give her what she wants or else you won't get what you want.

7. She only gives her husband sex periodically. Usually once each month. She will deny she does this if you ever point it out.

8. She wants joint credit card accounts without spending limits. NEVER AGREE TO THIS. Even a woman who is not a con artist can drain you dry this way. Just imagine what a con artist will do with this access to your money!

9. She lives her life by the "Three Questions of the custody determination". She always takes the kids to

the doctor. Appointments, urgent care, and the emergency room. In fact, she will likely take the kids to urgent care unnecessarily just so she can chalk up another time she took the kids to the doctor.

10. She always takes the kids to the dentist.

11. She NEVER takes the kids anywhere else. Ever. Not the circus, not the zoo, not camping, not to a ball game, not even to their own hockey practice. Anyone who has kids but never spends time with them is a con artist who had kids for money, for a house and child support.

12. When one of the kids is sick in the night, she insists that she be the one to stay up. She is adamant. If you are rocking the baby to get him to stop crying, she will wrestle him away from you before she will let you take credit for making him happy. No matter what, she will be the one up with the kids. The husband does not argue because he needs some sleep. She gladly stays up, with amphetamines, if necessary, because she knows about the three questions in a custody hearing. When the judge asks "Who stays up with the kids at night when they are sick?" she can say "Me!"

If you go to sleep and let her take care of the baby, then in her mind, she just won. Remember, the con artist keeps her eye on the ultimate prize: winning the custody battle. Her entire scheme depends on winning the custody battle.

Remember this: If you rent your home instead of buy it, she does not get a house. She might get child support and even spousal maintenance, but she can't get your house and all the equity.

13. Whenever one of her children skins his knee, she rushes to him and showers him with affection and sympathy. She will hug and kiss him and rock him until he feels better. She will then make a major production out of cleansing the wound and applying an antiseptic. She will then get him some chocolate milk.

14. After witnessing this a few times, you think "She is crazy." Not so. She is making sure that when the judge asks "Who do the children go to when they get hurt?" her answer will be "Me!" She gets angry at her husband if he plays golf, hockey, baseball, or softball. She gets angry if he goes hunting or running or if he sleeps late or works late or stops at the hardware store on his way home. She gets angry every time she has to watch the kids. If he is not home, then she has to watch the kids. A con artist only had the kids to make money. Watching them is aggravating to her. She will bitch long and loud about it every time until her husband breaks down and hires a nanny or simply quits doing anything he likes to do outside the house. Husbands of con artists often say "It just isn't worth it to leave the house. She bitches so much that it is easier to just stay home."

15. Her husband does not even argue with her anymore. He can't stand the noise. She has worn him out with her nagging, bitching and screaming. And she isn't even warmed up yet!

16. She is extremely jealous. She watches her husband like a hawk. Every time his gaze lands on another woman,

she says "You like what you see?" or "Something interesting at the next table?" or "My, what a lovely girl over there" always with plenty of sarcasm and some simmering anger.

17. She insists that her husband always come straight home after work. She becomes angry if she has to watch the kids for any amount of time.

18. She calls her husband at work and says, angrily, "When are you coming home?" between 3 and 5 days per week. In the morning, she says, "Do you think you can be on time for dinner tonight?"

19. She goes out Seven days per week. She shops compulsively. She visits friends. They go out to dinner. She is gone all day on Saturday and Sunday. She knows her husband is watching the kids, so it is fine for her to be gone. The children ask "Where is Mommy?" The children miss her. She does not care. When she has fun, it does not involve her husband or her kids.

20. She has a bag of tricks to transfer money from her husband to herself. For example: She lies and tells her husband that her wedding ring and engagement ring slipped off while she was doing the dishes or snorkeling in Hawaii. The rings went down the drain or down to bottom of the Ocean. An insurance claim is made and a check is written to the wife for the value of the rings. In fact, the rings are safe and sound in her dresser. Next, she has no taxes deducted from her paycheck. This makes her paycheck bigger and, at the end of the year, it will make her husband's tax refund smaller. She then expects him to give her half of his tax refund.

Next, when she goes to the grocery store, she writes a check for $80.00. The groceries only cost $50.00. She pockets $30.00 cash and tells her husband she spent $80.00 on groceries. He puts $80.00 into the grocery account. Next is the gas tank trick. The con artist occasionally trades cars with her husband. To impress her friends or to use his big trunk or whatever. She lets him use her car that day. The gas tank is almost empty. If she has to fill his car, she only puts in $5.00 worth. She knows that he will fill the tank of her car. She pulls this trick as often as possible.

21. She never talks to her husband except to bitch or tell him everything she needs him to buy for her. Then, suddenly, she will say "Hi honey. How was your day?" As if she cares.

22. It comes out like she read that she should say that once in a while. She is never happy to see her husband. She is angry at him always, no matter what he does to make her happy. He can try everything any expert suggests. None of them will work. The only exception to the rule is if he has just spent a large amount of money on her. If he is handing her something made of gold with some diamonds, she will smile at him. If they are currently on a European vacation and he is paying for everything, then she will smile at him. A con artist may even like her husband for that short time while they are touring Europe or when the gifts are being delivered. Unscheduled sex is even possible.

23. Her gratefulness and joy disappear before the Sun comes up the next day after you give her an expensive

gift. One day after returning home from a fabulous vacation, she is back to her old self. Angry, covetous, jealous, and bossy.

24. She likes money, a lot, but she doesn't want to have to work.

[Note: These are the clues I know about. I am sure there are more.]

Chapter Six

It's Never Too Late to Start Protecting Yourself from Divorce

If you have a wife who does some or all of the things listed in Chapter 5, paragraphs 1 through 24, you might receive a Divorce Summons in the next few years. If you have been living with these behaviors for a long time, you might decide to serve your wife with a Divorce Summons sooner than that. Either way, you need to start your preparations to minimize the losses you could suffer in a divorce. Here are some suggestions:

1. Buy a second house and use it as rental property. This makes a nice investment if your wife never divorces you and it gives you a place to live if she does. If you try to buy a new house after a divorce, you will find lenders will not loan you any money.

2. Start stashing money. Anything is better than nothing. Being left penniless by a female judge is a real possibility. Don't let it happen to you. Go on a fishing trip to Wisconsin and drive right to Sault St. Marie, Ontario, Canada. Open an account with a Canadian brokerage. Cash out some mutual funds or life insurance policies and bring the money with you to Canada.

3. Get frugal. The dollar you save today is the dollar you

will have after the Judge takes every Dollar she thinks you have. Don't spend all your money on golf clubs when the wife makes sure you can never play golf anyway. Don't fly south twice every winter. Let your wife know that she should fly south with her girlfriends and that you really hate to waste time sitting in the Sun. Make it clear that she can pay for her own trips. Another thing, stop spending several Thousand Dollars each year on lunch. Please, be smarter than that.

4. Be smart about where you put your secret money. Every account you have in your name in the United States will show up on a credit check. Make sure your secret investments do not show up on a credit check. Do not hide anything valuable in a safe deposit box. That is the first thing they will look for. Make sure the mail and statements go to your work address. Your wife reads your mail, in case you didn't know.

5. Remember, a secret is a secret. Don't tell people about the hidden money. It only takes one person telling your ex-wife about your secret stash for the court to take every last cent and leave you in real trouble. The real villain in this story is the court system. The predator in a dress merely benefits from the Court's conduct.

6. Never admit to the Court you have the hidden money. If the Judge asks you "Do you have any assets you have not disclosed?" you have to be able to look her in the eye and say "No your honor". You need guts to survive a divorce. If you can't fight for your money, maybe you don't deserve to keep any of it anyway.

7. Remember, if all your money is gone, you won't even be able to pay the child support and spousal maintenance. If you don't make those two payments, the judge can have you arrested and put in jail. Over and over. THIS IS SERIOUS. It's you against the legal system. If you want to keep anything after a divorce, you have to be smart, quick, and tough.

8. Never feel guilty about trying to keep some money for yourself. Remember, you may end up using all the money to pay child support and spousal maintenance anyway. Divorce laws are unfair from beginning to end. The Judges are biased in favor of women. Female judges are so biased that they seem to be attorneys representing your ex-wife. The amount of child support and spousal maintenance is not based on actual income. It is based on "Earnings Capacity". A judge can order a man to pay his ex-wife More Than He Earns. A man can tell the complete truth to the judge and be labeled a liar anyway. A man can end up in jail because he simply does not earn enough to meet the obligations the Court has placed upon him.

Meanwhile, the ex-wife gets custody of the children. She sits comfortably in a house she never made a payment on during the marriage. She counts all of her money she gets without having to work. She can get a job if she wants to have more spending money, or not. It is up to her.

Divorce Courts treat men like criminals while treating women like royalty. Anyone who would begrudge a man a little financial security has no sense of fairness at all.

Here is something to ponder: A man who is irresponsible and runs up credit card debts he can never repay is safe from his creditors. His creditors cannot take his homestead or any of his furniture. They cannot take his car or any of his retirement savings. They cannot even garnish his wages if he declares Bankruptcy and wipes out the debts. He is safe. **NONE OF THOSE THINGS ARE SAFE FOR A MAN IN A DIVORCE.** The Court can take his homestead, his furniture, his car, and all of his retirement income and Bankruptcy cannot help him. The law provides a man with a wife and kids with no financial security at all. A stash of secret money is his only chance at security.

Chapter Seven

Understanding Divorce Law

Understanding divorce law is essential to protecting yourself from it. All debutantes, gold diggers, and con artists are intimately familiar with it long before you meet them. Every man considering marriage should be required to learn about divorce law before he walks down the aisle. Legally, it would be better for a man not to get married because getting married is what brings him under the jurisdiction of a divorce court judge who can't wait to invade every account, he has in order to hand the money to his ex-wife.

Of course, telling a man not to get married is a waste of breath. The fact is, a man in love will take on all the risks of marriage in hopes of being in a happy marriage with happy children running through the house.

Divorce laws are not fair. They were never intended to be. They were created to protect innocent women from unethical men. Divorce laws protect women by enforcing the bargain inherent in marriage. The marriage bargain is essentially this: The woman will have sex with one man exclusively and on a regular basis in return for his financial support and his promise to never leave her without adequate food, shelter and clothing for herself and her children.

Divorce Court is where Divorce laws are interpreted and applied. All Divorce Court rulings are enforced by the Sheriff and police. You know, the police? They are those guys with badges who have the authority to beat, tazer, mace and shoot you if you resist them.

Divorce Court has no jurisdiction over anyone who does not get married. When a man gets married, he voluntarily subjects himself to the jurisdiction of the Divorce Court. Every application for a marriage license should bare this warning: "Warning, getting married may one day result in a divorce court judge taking all of your property, every penny you ever saved and every penny you will ever earn and jailing you anyway for not paying enough money to your ex-wife. The judge may make a factual finding that everything you say is a lie, limit your access to your children, take away your passport, garnish your wages, seize your tax refunds and award your ex-wife thousands of dollars in attorney fees if you so much as present an argument on your own behalf. A judge may make findings of fact which are not true and have you arrested by a bailiff if you object too much. The judge can have you jailed if she decides you violated one of her orders, even if you do everything in your power to comply. Granted, that is a worst-case scenario, but it is a possibility of which you should be aware."

In case you were wondering "how can the judge order you to pay more money than you make?" The answer is: By calling you a liar and finding as a matter of fact that you have undisclosed income. If you are self-employed when the divorce papers are filed, this will likely happen to you. Your ex-wife will claim you make more money than you admit and the

Judge will believe her even if there is no supporting evidence and it is obvious to you that your ex is a con artist.

All of these things have happened in America and they will all happen again. This week. If you get married, these things can happen to you. If you do not get married, they can't. **DIVORCE COURT JUDGES HAVE NO JURISDICTION OVER YOU UNLESS YOU GET MARRIED.**

One way to protect yourself from the unfairness of divorce laws is to simply never get married. Problem solved, worries gone.

The problem with that approach is that you might like to have a traditional marriage. You may want a wedding and honeymoon and kids and a house with a yard and to grow old with a woman you love. Passing up a good woman for fear that she is a con artist would be tragic. For you, another solution is needed. Thank goodness, there is one.

Go ahead and get married. Just make sure you have a safety net. What you need is a secret stash of money. The more, the better. To a married man with children, hidden money is the only form of security. You also need the guts to lie under oath. When a judge asks you if you have disclosed all of your assets, you must say "Yes, I have". If you can't do that, then you really should not get married! If you tell them, you have hidden money, you can kiss it goodbye. When the judge strips you clean of all your money, you need something to break your fall.

Here are some good places to stash money: Canadian bank account, German, French and British government bonds,

British mutual Funds, your basement, your attic, your parents' house, buried in the woods at an exact longitude and latitude, in your filing cabinet in a long-closed file, in the biker boots your wife hates, in a Canadian safe deposit box. This is just the beginning of an endless list of possible spots.

Additionally, you need to know as much about divorce laws as the con artists, gold diggers and debutantes know. Trust me, they know plenty. They know as much about the rules of divorce as basketball fans know about the rules of basketball.

Draining money from men is what con artists do for a living. Divorce court is where the con artist shines. Divorce court is where all of her work pays off. She tailors her life to take advantage of the laws of divorce, child support and property distribution. She does this in much the same way as an investor tailor his investments to take advantage of tax laws, or an ambitious high school student tailor his life to get into the college of his choice.

A con artists has prepared for her day in court since before she met you. You need to prepare for the possibility that your wife or fiancé is conning you. If you do, and it turns out you married a good woman after all, there is no harm done. If you don't prepare and it turns out you married a con artist, you are doomed. Your standard of living will be destroyed. You will almost certainly take a financial beating from which you can never recover. You will be angry, bitter, and poor.

You will wonder how and why this can happen in America to an honest, kind, generous, faithful, hardworking, and generally wonderful husband and father. No one will even attempt to justify or explain it. That is the way it is. That is the way it will always be. The only thing a man can do about it is take the steps necessary to protect against it.

You have to stash away money. Get married with a nest egg your fiancé does not know about. Add to it during the marriage. Keep it secret. If retirement arrives and your wife is still with you, the both of you can share it. You see, a wife with a true heart loses nothing if you protect yourself from divorce. She comes out better off! A wife who sticks by you gets an unexpected benefit at the end.

You can successfully protect yourself from divorce. What follows is a list of Divorce Laws and Rules every man needs to know. Simply knowing the rules will allow you to recognize when your spouse is tailoring her behavior to maximize her take in a divorce and allow you to defeat her strategy. If you can defeat her strategy, you will not be left in financial ruin. You will be OK. If you win the custody battle, you will not lose your house. You will not pay child support; you will receive it! You will have avoided disaster and provided financial security for you and your children.

A. How child custody is determined
B. How child custody decisions affect property distribution
C. How child support is determined
D. How spousal maintenance is determined
E. How your income is determined
F. How assets are divided
G. How Court Orders are enforced
H. How to minimize your vulnerability

A. How child custody is determined

A man's lawyer presenting argument in a child custody hearing will argue that his client is an outstanding parent. He is kind, patient, friendly, happy, and sober. He is a good teacher and he loves his children. He has never hit any of them and he never will. The lawyer will present witnesses who have seen the man with his children and will testify that all of those claims are true.

A woman's lawyer will argue that his client is the one who takes the kids to the doctor and dentist, stays up with the kids when they are sick in the night, and she is the one the kids run to when they hurt themselves. Since these are the three things the judge wanted to know, the woman wins the hearing. She gets custody.

Officially, the Judge's mission is to create a parenting arrangement which best serves the needs of the children. A prenuptial agreement on custody of children or child support payments is unenforceable. All judges will sleep well at night if they simply award the mother custody every time. You have to be the exception if you want to be awarded custody.

Do not waste time trying to prove your ex-wife is a bad person or a bad mom. Simply make sure you are the one who takes the kids to the doctor and dentist, stays up with them in the night when they are sick, and make sure the kids know that a skinned knee will generate just as much care and love from you as it does from their Mom. Those three things will give you the best chance of winning custody, keeping your house, and having some disposable income after the divorce.

Answer these questions and you will know who gets custody of the children in a divorce:

1. Who takes the kids to doctor and dentist appointments?
2. Who gets up in the night with the kids when the kids are sick?
3. Who do the kids run to when they skin their knee?

When making a child custody determination, the judge asks the three questions and whichever parent gets named two out of three times wins. Whoever wins gets the kids, the house, the car, child support, and has a decent shot at spousal maintenance, especially if there are three or more kids. (Con artists always want to have three or more kids)

Every con artist knows these rules. The same way they know that wedding invitations need to match the bridesmaid dresses (Did you know that?). They have been learning this kind of thing since before they went on their first date. Most men are perfectly uninformed about these things. Most men have no idea what power they are giving some man-hater judge the moment the men sign the marriage license. If men were aware of this, they would REALLY get to know their girlfriends before proposing. Here is a rule ALL MEN MUST KNOW: The minute your wife gets bored of you or decides she likes your money better than she likes you, she can divorce you, get you removed from the house, prevent you from seeing your children for a while, have you spending all your vacation money on your lawyer and possibly hers, divest you of all ownership in your house, take your favorite car, and drain you of all disposable income for the rest of your life. She can leave you a sad, lonely, defeated financial wreck any time she wants. You don't even have to do anything wrong.

Let that sink in for a minute.

There will be many indicators if your wife is preparing to divorce you and leave you penniless (See chapter 5). If you see that your wife is setting you up, confront her. Tell her you love her and that she is much better off as your wife than she will be as your ex-wife. You are much better off however, if you take steps to protect yourself in the first place (see chap. 7)

A telltale sign that your wife is preparing to win custody in a divorce is if she insists on always being the one to take the kids to the dentist and doctor appointments. She even takes the kids to urgent care a little more often than necessary just to chalk up another time she took them to the doctor. No man should allow that pattern to develop. Go to every Doctor and Dentists appointment your children ever have! If your wife insists on coming too, if your wife insists that she go instead of you, or if she argues and insists that you not take the kids to the doctor's office, I guarantee she is setting you up.

A telltale sign that your wife is preparing to win custody in a divorce is if she insists on being up with the kids every time they get sick in the night. Resist the temptation to go back to bed. If your wife refuses to share the sick duty with you, I guarantee she is setting you up.

A telltale sign that your wife is preparing to win custody in a divorce is if she goes overboard in fawning over the kids every time they skin their knee. If she never tells them to get tough and stop crying, if she makes skinning their knee an event which results in untold showers of affection and tender loving care, the kids will naturally go to her when they are sick or hurt. This is especially true if she ignores them all the rest of the time. If your wife does this, I guarantee she is setting you up.

If you see this pattern, I guarantee your wife is setting you up. You cannot sit by idly and allow this. You have to insist on caring for the kids in these instances. Insist that you be allowed to nurture and reassure the kids when they are truly hurting. Never say something like "Stop babying him" when your wife is showering your whimpering child with affection. If you do that, you may as well hand over your keys to the house, car, and boat right then and there. That is exactly what the con artists hopes you will say.

B. How Child Custody Decisions Affect Property Distribution

Whomever gets custody of the kids gets the house and all of its furniture and appliances. After that, the Judge totals up all the property and its value and divides it the way he thinks fair and equitable. If a man hopes for half the assets or more, he has to win the custody battle. If the husband makes the money and the wife stays home with the kids, she will likely get a large portion of the assets even if she got the house, furniture, appliances and a car. In theory, the husband is supposed to get half the assets. In reality, the wife gets more than half. You will have to have a large stash of money just to come away with half the total assets. This, in spite of the fact that it was your earnings that paid for all of the assets. Remember, fairness is not required in Divorce Court and "Fair and equitable" is just code for

"However the judge wants". Judges do not respond favorably to the argument "I earned all the money that paid for the assets so I should get more than half of the assets" If you say that in court, the judge will be thinking "You will be lucky if I give you any portion of the assets, sonny"

If you wonder "Why would a judge be hostile to me?" The answer is because judges are hostile to all men and some women too. I don't know why. They all seem just a little fed up with presiding over divorce cases.

C. How child support is determined

Most states use a calculation that takes the income of both parents into account as well as the percentage of time each has custody during the year. You simply enter the numbers in the formula and it tells you how much the non-custodial parent will pay in child support. The most anyone ever has to pay in any state is around $2,250.00 per month. If a woman wants more than that, she will have to get spousal maintenance. To get that, she has to get married and divorced first.

If a man makes $80,000 or more, he pays $2,250 per month in child support. If he makes more than that, there is no increase in his child support. If a man makes between $0 and $79,000 per year, he pays something between $0 and $2,200 per month in child support. Child support obligations change when a man's income changes. A man can expect to pay between 15% and 35% of his income or earning capacity in child support.

It should be noted that no one can afford to pay child support. We all know how hard it is to get by on 100% of our income. Try getting by on 68% of your income (especially after you have lost your house, all your equity and half your savings.)

D. How spousal maintenance is determined

Many divorces have no spousal maintenance order. Judges award it when a couple has been married a long time and the husband earned more money than his wife. Essentially, spousal maintenance is awarded to prevent a stay-at-home wife from suffering a drastic drop in her standard of living due to a divorce. So, if your wife has been living very well off your income for 17 years, you will probably owe spousal maintenance. If the wife can provide nicely for herself, no spousal maintenance will be awarded. If a man seeks spousal maintenance, he can forget it.

Unlike child support, there is no limit to spousal maintenance. To their credit, most judges are conservative in handing out spousal maintenance awards. "25% of the ex-husband's income for 5 years" might be a typical award. Insist that your wife be employed and productive and you won't have to worry about paying spousal maintenance.

E. How your income is determined

If you have a salary and you have your tax returns for the past Ten years, the Court will declare your income to be your actual income or more. The Court may determine that you should be making more. If you just tried harder for promotions and worked some overtime, your income would be higher. If the Judge thinks you are intentionally making less than you, could he will refer to your "earnings capacity" instead of your income. If you earn a salary, you have the best chance of the Court accurately determining your income.

If your income is different every year, the judge will likely treat your best year ever as your income. The Judge may average the past Five years. If you are self-employed and you have tax returns for the past Ten years, and the Judge believes what you say then your income is your income. However, if the Judge believes your ex-wife, you are in trouble. I guarantee she will tell the Court you make way more money than you admit. If things go really bad, you could end up owing more spousal maintenance and child support than you actually earn. An impossible situation. This could land you in jail. You may have to live in another country just to stay out of jail.

My advice, if you are self-employed and love it, is to have an accountant do your taxes. Or, sell your business and get a job if you are married to a greedy little thing.

F. How assets are divided

Assets are, in theory, divided half and half between the husband and wife. In reality, this rarely happens. The assets are most often split unevenly with the woman getting the larger share. Typically, the one making the largest income gets less property. Property can be a little like unofficial spousal maintenance. Over time, the woman can sell the extra assets to help her raise money. Sometimes the asset the woman receives is money and is therefore indistinguishable from spousal maintenance. The decision on how the property will be divided belongs to the judge. She has discretion to make property divisions which are fair and equitable. Of course, when a judge is biased, "Fair and equitable" is neither fair nor equitable.

G. How Court Orders are enforced

When a judge makes an order, it has the power of law. It will be obeyed or else it will be enforced by the County Sheriff. City police may also be employed to enforce a Court Order. This includes all orders of any kind. Child custody, possession of the house, ownership of the house. Signatures on Deeds and no contact orders. All of them have the force of law and disobeying one is Contempt of Court. Being held in Contempt of Court gets you arrested and held in jail for as long as the judge thinks appropriate.

H. How you can minimize your vulnerability

First, decide not to be a victim. Get tough. A man with a lot of money has to be tough enough to keep it just like a kid with a candy bar has to be tough enough to keep it. If the laws of your state are unfair to you, then be a rebel. Don't let anyone scheme against you. When the kids have a doctor appointment, you take them. When the kids are sick in the night, you get up with them. When one of the kids skins his knee, you tend to him and make him feel better. Those three things control the outcome of the custody hearing and the outcome of the custody hearing controls the outcome of the divorce.

In case your wife files for divorce, are you going to get custody of the children, keep your house and its equity, receive child support instead of paying it, and walk away from the courthouse owing no spousal maintenance? Or is your ex-wife going to get everything, leaving you wondering how you are going to afford food? You can decide how it will be. Even if you get a bad outcome in court, are you capable of saving up a stash of money to take care of you?

Realize that married fathers of young children have NO FINANCIAL SECURITY. They can provide financial security for their wife and kids, but the laws of Divorce prevent security for the man. Get mad about that! Think of whoever made the rules of Divorce as your personal enemy. Do not feel any obligation to play the game by their rules. They are so unfair and one sided as to constitute gender-based discrimination. What goes on in divorce courtrooms everyday violates federal and state anti-discrimination statutes.

You need to hide some money to live off of should the divorce disaster ever strike you. Hidden money is just savings for married men. Their chance at security. Sell your house and rent a house for the family. A con artist will have a fit over this move. Keep your car for a long time. When it quits, replace it with a used car. Stash the savings somewhere safe. Get frugal. Save your money until you have enough hidden away to live on in the event that the wife and the Court System decide to take all of your money from you.

You may ask "Don't I have to declare all of my assets to the Court? My answer to that is "If you want to give away all of your money and be left penniless, go ahead. But if you've got a backbone and a little fight in you, keep a secret or two."

You may wonder "Where should I stash the money?" The answer is "Anywhere you can be sure to get it back". It is a great big world. You could hide it in your fathers' desk drawer, a cave in Colorado, a bank in Argentina, a brokerage firm in London, your best friend's garage. You could invest in foreign bonds. You could use your Dad's address for the secret accounts so that your wife does not learn about them by reading your mail. You could put the money in your Dad's account at a bank and he could leave the account contents to you in his will. (Inherited money is not a marital asset) You could have a savings account in Paris and one in Rome. You could buy lots of gold and keep it in a safe at you mom's house. You know, anywhere. Hire a private investigator to tell you the hardest place to find stashed money.

Chapter Eight

The Good News Protecting Yourself from Unfair Divorce Laws and the Con Artists who Depend on them.

There are many ways to fully protect yourself from divorce laws. Here are some good ones.

1. Never buy a house. Rent instead. Amazingly, this solves everything! Remember, the con artist intends to get a house and child support and spousal maintenance. If you don't buy a house, she doesn't get one when she divorces you. If you don't buy a house, she will beg and plead, she will give you all kinds of arguments for home ownership. She will tell you how great it will be to have a garden and a big dog. She will tell you children need a house and she won't have children until you buy a house. She will promise great sex in every room, she will threaten no sex ever again. Finally, she will just divorce you and try the con on someone else. By the way, renting is a very good idea. Renters never buy furnaces, storm windows, lawn mowers, snow blowers, new siding, air conditioning, or new roofs. They don't even have to pay heat or electric bills. Not a bad deal. Any wife who is not a con artist will agree, renting is the better option.

2. Never get married. If you don't get married, Divorce judges have no power over you. They can make you pay child support but they can't take your house, car or life savings. Many couples have long happy lives together without ever getting married. Think about it.

3. Never get divorced. Instead, buy a little house by the water for your little con artist and pay her bills. She can live there and spend her time however she wants. That is what she really wants anyway. A nice home with no bills. This is way less expensive than a divorce that goes badly. Plus, you made a nice real estate investment.

4. Win the custody battle. Con artists depend on their husbands giving up and never having a custody battle. Surprise everyone and win it. Be the parent that takes the kids to the doctor and dentist. Be the parent who stays up in the night with the kids when they are sick. Be the parent the kids run to when they get hurt. Two can play at this game. Even a biased judge will have a hard time giving the wife custody when the judge's own test says the husband should get custody.

5. Be extremely wealthy. If the property was yours before the wedding, it is non-marital property and it will not be divided up if there is a divorce. You get to keep it.

6. Be extremely poor. You won't lose any property in a divorce and your child support payments will be low.

7. Stash enough money to live on. Plus, a little more. Never tell anyone about it but your Dad or Mom. Remember, this is war. The con artist is after your last nickel. She does not contribute a dime to the

household. Don't let her get away with every dime you can save. If your wife is not a con artist, then the stash will provide financial security for both of you. A stash is a good idea no matter who you marry. After all, there is no law requiring us to blow every dime we earn, Is there? If your wife does not know about the savings, she won't refuse to give you sex until you hand her the money.

8. Keep a diverse collection of assets. Do not sink all of your money into your house. Have an equal amount in retirement funds, Stock portfolios, mutual funds and rental real estate. Don't let your wife talk you in to buying such an expensive house that you are made house poor as a result. [Note: this advice is for men who won't follow my advice to just rent their home.] Con artists always try to convince their mark (husband) to buy a bigger, more expensive house than the one they have.

9. Insist that your wife get educated and employed. Insist that she grow up and quit spending every dollar she has. Insist that she invest her money in retirement funds, stock portfolios, mutual funds and rental real estate. Insist that she stop spending all her time shopping. Tell her to spend a little time with her children instead. If you can get her to do this, the Court will decide she is self-sufficient and that she does not need spousal maintenance. The Court will then give you a bigger share of the marital property and you won't have to pay any spousal maintenance!

If your wife refuses to cooperate, confront her. Tell her

she has no right to put the burden of securing her futures all on you.

This method of protecting yourself from a con artist is preferable. You could turn a lazy thief into an honest, productive human being.

10. Simply inform the con artist that you are on to her and demand that she stops it. How dare she marry you just so she can divorce you and take your money? How dare she scheme against you, constantly hold sex hostage, treat you like a servant and actively prepare for a custody battle for a divorce that need never happen? How dare she insist that you never leave the house and refuse to watch the kids long enough for you to play golf once a week? What makes it OK for her to try to get away with this? Why doesn't she start acting like a human being and start treating her husband like one?

Who knows? This just might work. The biggest hurdle will be the con artist's refusal to ever admit anything. If she denies it, you could list for her all of the things she is doing that scream "Con Artist" and simply ask her to stop doing those things (see chapter 5," How to recognize a con artist").

11. Be very careful who you marry. Don't marry a girl who seems driven by greed. Don't marry a woman who speaks of nothing but diamonds, minks, and Mercedes Benzes. Marry a woman with actual values. Someone who does not judge others by the price of their clothing. Women who maintain an ongoing critique of other people's clothes and cars are most likely to be con artists. They are most likely to be a predator in a dress.

Even if they are not scheming to divorce you and take your house, they are still the type who will treat you like a thing they can shake money out of. They will drain you of all your money in order to pay for the consumer goods they must have.

Chapter Nine

Summary

When a couple gets divorced, usually the wife gets the kids, the house, child support and spousal maintenance. That much money for no work is very attractive. It causes some women to get married, spend their husband's money, have a couple of children and then divorce their husband. They expect to get the kids, the house, some of the husband's retirement savings, child support and spousal maintenance. Pretty good for a girl who never held a job in her life.

I call a woman who plans to carry out this scheme a Predator in a Dress. I refer to the scheme as a con job. The con artist's mark is any wealthy man. The con is simple. The con artist pretends to be in love with the wealthy man. He buys it and the wedding is set. Ten years later, they have a nice house, two kids and no savings. She divorces him, hoping to get the house free and clear, with a steady income too! She is awarded custody of the kids, the house (she picked it out herself), monthly child support and monthly spousal maintenance.

The con worked like a charm and she is still young enough to do it again. Meanwhile, her ex-husband is in financial ruin. He never saw it coming. He has no idea what hit him and no clue how he could have protected himself. Now he lives to see his kids every other weekend and can't afford to go many places with them because he has no disposable income.

This scheme should be a crime. Oddly, it has the full support of the Judicial System and Legislature of all fifty states. Don't let it happen to you. There are ways you can see this coming (see chapter 5). There are things you can do to protect yourself (see chapter 7). You owe it to yourself and your children to do everything you can to protect yourself from the Predator in a Dress.

THE END

Tips To Remember

- If you or your wife file a divorce Petition with the Court, you will have a judge assigned to your case. If the judge is female, immediately file a Notice of Removal. This will get you a different judge and, you hope, a male.

- Never allow your wife to be a stay-at-home mom or a full-time homemaker.

- Take your children to at least half of all doctor and dental appointments by yourself. If the wife comes every time, make sure you are there every time as well.

- Never allow your wife to be up with sick kids any more than you are.

- Make sure to match your wife cuddle for cuddle every time your kids get sick or hurt.

- Get a job. Being self-employed is disastrous if you get divorced. Your income will be grossly overstated by the Judge and you could end up with a child support and spousal maintenance obligation which is higher than your actual income.

- Every time your wife says "I do all the work around here" calmly point out that she does not do all the work around here. Point out that vacuuming a clean carpet does not even count as work. Nor does shopping or gardening.

- If you get married, plan on seeking custody of the children in the event of a divorce.

- Never buy more house than you can comfortably afford. Placing all your equity in the one asset that your wife is likely to get in a divorce is not a good decision. If the family can only afford one house after a divorce, then only one parent is going to live in a house. Guess who that is going to be.

- Make sure you have liquid assets sufficient to buy a second house to match the first in the event of a divorce. The con artist will insist on the most expensive house possible. You must insist on the most financial security possible.

- Insist that your wife works and contributes to the mortgage, utilities, phone bill, cable bill, etc. Resist the temptation to be the beast of burden to make her happy. That could turn around and bite you later, in the form of spousal maintenance.

www.ingramcontent.com/pod-product-compliance
Lightning Source LLC
Chambersburg PA
CBHW042124050526
44539CB00056B/1849